EVE AND OTHER
Acts of Defiant Gratitude

To Yehuda —
an old friend,
a good friend,
an always friend.

poems by
Timothy Donohue

Tim

10-28-19.

Cover Photograph by Timothy Donohue
Cover Design by Jennifer Leigh Selig

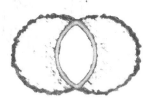

MANDORLA BOOKS
WWW.MANDORLABOOKS.COM

"To get the full value of joy you must have someone to divide it with. After all these years I see that I was mistaken about Eve in the beginning; it is better to live outside the Garden with her than inside without her."

~Mark Twain

"How wonderful that we have met with a paradox. Now we have some hope of making progress."

~Niels Bohr

"Forget heroin. Just try giving up irony, that deep-down need to mean two things at once, to be in two places at once, not to be there for the catastrophe of a fixed meaning."

~Edward St. Aubyn

CONTENTS

PART I

PART II

PART III

PART IV

PART I

Defiant Acts Of Gratitude

Eve made
heavenly salvation
all about earthly choices

Clearly spelled out
by a Creator
who created her

from another guy…
or so the story goes

But we know
that in the syntax
of the soul

there is no handwriting
that misspells
our desire

to share ourselves with another, to become love

It cost us
this continuously ending
here and now

but here we are
still choosing
passion and joy

still practicing
all these defiant acts
of gratitude

Rita On Her Day Off With A Book Of Poetry

Rita stared at page one, poem one,
got to the third stanza, looked up and said
"Where's the 'on' button to this thing?"

Maybe it's that idea in the second line,
the one about "bitterness that leaves
a chemical taste in your mouth"

I offered that up to Rita, but since I was in another poem
("Untitled") 17 pages away, she heard me but couldn't see me...

Rita wrestled with that idea
for a minute or so, flipping
it up and down—like a light switch.

She got up and turned off the music
playing in the kitchen and her bedroom.
And she took off her shoes, thinking

the comfort of slippers will crack
open this poem like a coconut and fill me
with fresh sweet coconut milk

She started over. This time it was different.
The book seemed light in her fingers,
Her clothes seemed to loosen around her body

Her breathing shortened to gasps, until:
"Be quiet. Sit still. You will be unborn
to the circumstances at hand."

What clever cleavage, Rita thought.
Still, it's silly to sit here being unborn on my day off
The errands to run, the soup to make...

I'll read more on Sunday

Hypoxia

Nothing
Stays put

The water
The planets
The stars
The heart...

What keeps moving
Cannot be accumulated

There is no museum
Of breathing.

What happens here
Is the first draft

Of who we think we are...
Until hypoxia sets in,

And then we slide ourselves,
Like an essay, under an eternal door

And move on...

Photocopies

If we photocopy our actions
each time according to our definitions
of want and need, we will miss

The picture not taken.

———

If we listen to each other, waiting
to see the breath of our own voice
in the mirror of another's face, we will miss

The word not heard.

———

If we forge our love,
the way some forge paintings
and passports, we will miss

The taste of Joy.

Distance

Distance can arrive slowly
or it can run red lights and stop signs
just to get home before you

Distance buys new clothes
hoping they might point another
towards a kind word

Distance reads a book
Distance takes a long walk
Distance sprinkles silence on food

It's distance that turns down a television
to say "You seem so distant lately.
Did we do something wrong?"

And it's distance that snaps
"What are you talking about.
I was watching that. What?"

Distance can dye your favorite skirt
the wrong color—right in front
of all your friends at a party

And it's distance that confirms
your new haircut looks nothing
like what you thought it would

Archimedes was right about
a straight line being the shortest
distance between two points

But I was wrong to keep pointing it out

Good Morning Mr. Donohue

Falling fast now
Between the walls of here
And vanished

Long held beliefs
Rot in a field of late-night promises
And a silly series of goals

Drop quickly from my inverted pockets

A thirst on top of a thirst sits in my mouth
As someone stands in my doorway
Staring at me with impunity

I pull a mask out of a drawer
That smells like cigarettes and martinis
I sip a cup of black coffee

Good morning Mr. Donohue
Good morning Mr. Donohue
Good morning Mr. Donohue

Good morning whoever you are

The Library (Funny Thing)

In the time of our troubles,
when your therapist made us
wear one mitten and one
surgical glove to work,
I began to record your laughter
secretly. In the theater.
When you were on the phone.
Twice while you were sleeping
and once when I said "I love
all the unreturned books
in your mind."

———

Work began in the library at Eden.
It started the day a secret spoken
memo hung in a golden frame was
somehow copied, read and shredded.
Eternity, instantly became a time
clock. Morning meant you always had
somewhere to be. And long soft days
on colorful blankets became coffee
breaks and cold sandwiches
from unlicensed food trucks.

———

After laughter, your mouth
always tasted like chocolate and
lemonade. Kisses produced beautiful
children who really adored us—
even when they rolled on the floor
laughing at our choices in clothes
and vacation destinations.

———

The last days were the hardest. The trips
to the store with buckets of coupons.
The hair splitting and invisible dental decay.
The Library filed liens on our jobs,
and past teachers appeared at hearings
with attendance records and incomplete
assignments. When we laughed, we were
shown the door.

———

Thing is, we had no beginning
so this is not the end. What you thought
was my spirit, was only a book
with the pages cut out to hide
another book. One you couldn't
return when you were finished
with it. Funny thing. Funny thing.

Sorrow

Night comes, filling windows
Like cups of dark coffee
You want to drink alone

But sorrow finds your table
And asks to join you—sitting down
Before you can say "no"

Sorrow wants to talk
And you want to remove sorrow
Like a shirt

But you can't pull it over your head. It won't budge.

Sorrow won't shut up.
Sorrow with its infinite sentences of "Remember when…"
Sorrow with its face leaning over the table and whispering

I came here to find you
And I'm not leaving
Until I do

Closings And Openings

She closes every email with wishes
For "joy and wonder" above her name

Like a note on a gift...

As if my joy was her wish to grant
As if my wondering keeps her up at night

Who's to say out loud what things
We should wish for in our lives?

But there she is, in her open saffron robe
Saying exactly what I mean

Tour Maps

Starting from nowhere
All those years ago, we knew
No map could do us wrong.

I scanned travel brochures
And the travel channel for
People that looked like us

But you didn't buy the need
For optional tours.
So all the drinking,

The investments gone crazy,
And the heart attack, all happened
While others were at museums or rodeos...

Like many, our desires
Traveled by air, but our steps
Kept us grounded

Slowly we learned that
Arriving early or late
Made little difference

We paid for the affection
That all tourists can count on,
But being rich in joy

We always left large tips...

Morning. Decades later.
I hear your laughter
30 minutes after

I've said something
I can't remember saying.

I laugh too.

Later, we will remember
to look at tour maps.

In The Daydream Of The Piano Teacher

In the daydream
Of the piano teacher
No student can speak
Because their voices
Are left by the mailbox

In the daydream
Of the piano teacher
Pupils have no fingers
Because they vanished
In a blur of scales,
And allegros

You must drink from the piano
at least eight times a day...

The students always nod and smile,
She always plays along—
You see, I know you do

And with their fingerless
Hands at the ready,
They begin again and
Again, and again
Until a perfect hour
Of silence has passed

These Small Frames

Images not quite sure
Of focus, subjects
Taunting King Verb

Flashlights casting about in a world of shadows...

The Book says
Flesh follows words:
Neither of us can get here any other way

So here we are, you and I
Reading this and feeling
All crossed out

Then improved
Then disappointed, then deleted...
Flesh follows words:

To do this thing of ours
Is to feel disassembled
Is to want to leave

But we always stay
Until we're pulled all the way through
These small frames

That somehow, sometimes
Border on wonder

The Three Of Her

I knew a woman
Who gave birth to a life
That took her life away

Piece by piece

It started early—
The birth canal
Just wouldn't let go

And over the years,
One by one, piece by piece
She learned why

Her body resisted

Six surgeries by age eight
Screaming dreams
In a loop

The wheel of mental illness....
A psyche one degree off
Going round, and round, and round...

Trips to the asylum
To the court, to the tattoo parlor
The illustrated guide

To self-medication
To heroin, oxycodone, jail
And anonymous friends

The daily dirge of voices
More real than any world can be
Making fictions

Out of anyone or anything that gets in the way...

I knew a woman
Who I thought I knew before
Who I don't know at all

A woman who was born, unborn and reborn
Who lives on, for the three of her—
Only asking for a long blue pool of water

Warm sunlight, and a piano
That remembers her hands and her body
Before she gave birth

To someone else

AM Kindergarten 1959

And in this box
A large framed photo:
Small faces pressed
Against parts of trees
And melted sand

A slate in the far-right photo corner
Clears things up:
LAKEVIEW AM Kindergarten 1959
Miss Bellora

And sure enough, there you are,
A visitor in your own life.
Your head cocked
Self-consciously to the right

And all of us pressed
Under a barrier
We can see through,
But not out of,

Not then, not now…

1959, and you were there
You must have been--that's your class
That's Miss Bellora's red hair under the black and white

But you ask questions
That can't be answered :
What is the color of that enameled brick in the background?
Is that the crematorium of personal pronouns?

And on, and on….What helps is remembering

Every past has another past:
Birds once nested in the wood of a picture frame
A woman walked barefoot over sand,
Before it was glass

Every echo forgets its beginning

The Distractions

1.
It isn't like finding some obscure
Symbolic meaning, like say a syringe
In a haystack of fax machines

2.
It's more like driving around with hay
In the trunk of your car, and swearing
It came from a farm on the moon

3.
He desires to have his last breath smell like distractions
In a room filled with distractions—
The plan is to pay no attention at all

4.
She desires the same, but differently
Of course—a spiraling arc of pleasure,
The journey to inner space

5.
Desire keeps us guessing, and not in a good way
Not like predicting when a wave will reach
Our toes on a beach, or how long it should snow

6.
The discharge of invention
Inside an appetite for distraction—
Absorption, expansion, separation: The Milky Way

7.
Even without one eye closed
And a fairly good telescope,
We can see where things will end

In A Year Of Backward Glances

In a year of backward glances,
and time spent with lives lived
near the first war to end all wars,
I vowed to stop using every
cliché I couldn't understand.
I don't know what's good
for a goose. I don't know
what a gander is, nor where to
take it. I don't understand why
something exceptional would
resemble the knees of bees.
Do bees really have knees?
And if they do, isn't it likely
they have knee problems?
And so on and so forth...
So I took all the clichés
I didn't understand and
put them in containers.
I then walked them to
the Do Not Enter site
in my mind. I could hear
them talking in the boxes
as I slowly set them down.
There were denouncements
and accusations. There were
warnings and such. As I was
leaving, there was a question
about cremation. I didn't stop
or look back. I just lied.
Said I couldn't understand.

The Early Birds

Robins hear
Frequencies of the invisible
In almost no light

Before dawn
On my lawn

Worms roar
Like freight trains
In their ears

The Poles Bend Toward Each Other

The crawl to stand, the drag to Forward, to the unknown
The wobbly scrape and pitch to the ground at the end
Start to finish, from here to gone
The poles bend toward each other

The first of life, the early years
The pocket-sized world of middle age
The blood building the brain
The blood looking for a place to stop

The birthing bed, the deathbed
The poles bend toward each other...

The poles bend toward each other
Until they break free and fall away
The poles bend toward each other
Until we drag ourselves Forward

To a second nativity
Of the unknown

A Few Lines About Disappointment

This poem will not do tricks for you
No matter what the reviews on the box say

The lines will disappoint you
Expectations on insight: denied
Thoughts on beauty: ridiculed

And that beloved childhood pet
Will stay underground

This line and the rest won't rhyme
And the meter will muddle
And make you want to cough

Yet here you are, ten lines in…
What are you looking for anyways?
Something you've lost?

Or is it something you've found?
Something you don't dare speak of?
Click on the agreement:

Neither of these things will occur.

It's true, I've had access to your thoughts for years,
I found the old ideas you put out in your trash can, and
stored them in my garage
But there's nothing for you to see here

You want a poem
That works like a pill
And delivers fast, fast, fast relief

You want to recreate those tears you left
At three funerals and your neighbor's second wedding
To not-you, again

Deep down, all men want something
That they think only the feminine can give:
Whether it's in them, or breathing next to them

So here you are, lingering after work,

Carrying a backpack
Into The Google Library
Of Failed Desires

Where you stay
Until they hand you this

After Further Review

1.
The ruling that joy is impossible
Is overturned. The player
Was in full possession of it
And never went out of bounds.
Put 50 years back on the clock.

2.
After review, the ruling that
Old school cloak rooms hid
Nothing but coats and
Winter boots is overturned.
Replay ninth grade.

3.
The ruling on the field is that the receiver
Was incapable of holding on to love
When he reached the end zone.
The ruling stands. What an ass.
Game over.

It Goes Without Saying

We come into the world
Without an alphabet
And leave with sentences
Stuffed in pockets
Of clothes we won't wear anymore

Aging brings conversations
With old photographs--
One-way professions of love,
Mumbled admissions of guilt,
And tea leaf readings
Of handwritten letters
All postmarked "Year Of Opportunity"

Moments past are moments lost
Until only a forever silence is near—
Then you want to unroll your alphabet
Then you want to scream "I was wrong"
Then you want to whisper "I love you"

But a charity comes round
To pick up those old clothes
And like you, it all goes
Without saying

Space Suites

In our space suites
We ended up on planets

Where breathable air recoiled
From touches of rain and snow

And mulishly refused
To enter our four lungs

The Lives Of The Silent

We met years later.
So much had not happened
Between and in-between us.

But we lost count of all that.

――――

The waiter brought two heavy lockboxes
With sentences inside. Sentences we rehearsed
For decades. Complete with notes on inflection

And when to lean forward or backward.

――――

All our endings are the same.
They're always about reaching silence
With no chance of return.

――――

I have depersonalized the last words
You said to me. I kept the word "need"
But switched the personal pronouns around.

I did the same with "hate."

――――

Nothing, is a gift.
You laugh. But it's true.
Nothing creates a gratitude
That makes no demands on you:

There's nothing to return.

Envelopes Of Words

-Genesis 2:20

You woke up
wondering, "Who gets to
name the stars?"

And I, somewhere between
the world of "I don't know"
and sleep

Said (dreamt?)

"No one."

Then thought (dreamt?)
about God telling Adam
to name all the animals

in the Garden of Eden...

And (woke up?) wondering
about a Supreme Being
who needed envelopes

to sort out creation

The Patriot

I'm a patriot, he said. I'm a patriot, he said again. He meant himself. Himself answering no one's question. But I was in the room. Two stools down. Coffee and scrambled eggs. The waitress didn't turn around, so I guess my ears were the target. I imagined him somewhere else, rolling out of bed, eating a bowl of Lucky Charms, then putting his pants on and smoking one of the cigarettes he told his wife and daughter he quit. They were gone. They left after he got angry and shot a newsman in the face on their almost new television. Now he's down to a phrase he repeats to anyone near him. The war he will always be in, unlike the wars he was never in, will never be over. The flag he loves, doesn't know his name. And I don't want to.

Prometheus v. Eve

Prometheus. Culture hero. Credited with making man out of clay. Stealing fire from a sunny day. Please. More men with pens and lyres telling stories to buck them up whenever they lost a battle or ran out of wine. But Eve. Now that's another story. Told by the Gardener to stay away from the tree of delicious apples, she thought it over. Talking to herself in the garden, to a part of her that seemed both of her and not-her. (This was confusing and awkward; something Adam couldn't deal with in himself.) But this tree. It looked good, bright blossoms then apples. It seemed to promise something that Eve just couldn't quite put her tongue on, standing there looking inside the locked orchard gate, with "Stay Out" written above the entrance. So she picked the lock on the gate, grabbed the closest apple and took a bite. The juice welled up around the corners of her lips and ran down her chin to her breasts. And it was good. It was *really good*. It tasted like everything in the garden. It tasted like a perfect moment and all the perfect moments to come. It tasted like everything she ever saw in the garden. It tasted like the present and the future. It tasted like things seen and things not seen. Strange and sweet. Slightly sour and crisp. She heard the crunch and felt the sweetness deep inside her. Everything smelled damp and green, like the sea. Eve had an idea that they could make life from life. She found Adam and told him what happened. She said she found four seeds inside the apple. She said they both had two seeds each—in their hand, and inside them. She said they could make more apples, and more of themselves. So they did. They ate many more sweet apples and made many more of themselves, until they found the garden to be too small for them all. So they left the garden, and the pissed-off Gardener. They went forth and made what we call the world. Now that's the truth. And it will be the truth no matter what the Greeks say. (Remember, they're tricky; always have been.) Next time you see a woman, be sure to say "Thanks, thanks for everything." Be grateful.

Sir Real And The Earl Of Sandwich

Sir Edwin Real, the Eighth Duke of Chum, was the first cousin of John Montagu, the Fourth Earl of Sandwich. They were out ale-housing when Sir Real, witnessed Montagu instructing a publican to serve him a piece of meat placed between two pieces of bread. He gave half to his cousin, and both were pleased with the taste, and the way the meal could be consumed without a spoon or fork. When others saw this quick feed-option, they said "I'll have what Sandwich and that Chum are having!" This gave Sir Real the idea of opening fast food shoppes throughout England, Scotland, and the colonies. He called these highway stands "The Sandwich Shoppe" and sold shares in the franchise to local hog farmers and bakery owners. Soon he was sued by his cousin for "fair and just compensation." The court in Kent delayed the hearing, however, due to a touch of plague in the area. This infuriated Sir Sandwich, who saw "neither man and nor woman" with "fever nor boil" near his estate. Consequently, the men decided to arbitrate the grievance by duel near a small orchard of apple trees. It took three rounds of fencing to declare Sir Real the winner. But as a sign of family being more important than franchise, the Duke of Real agreed to change the name (and menu) to "The Sandwich and Chum Shoppe". Soon there were more than 200 locations in fishing towns up and down the island's coastline, and in the colonies. The Earl of Sandwich died just before the 200th location was opened, but Sir Real honored his cousin, a former Admiral in His Majesty's Navy, by having the motto of the Sandwich family printed on all Sandwich and Chum food wrappers— *"After so many shipwrecks a haven."*

Where The Tears And The Antelope Play

There was a boy who listened to music, long before he memorized the alphabet. Ear was *all*. He saw things the way he heard them, not the way they were written or spelled. Tennessee Ernie Ford sang to him about loading sixteen tons of coal, but owing his immortal soul to pay for what a company stole. He tried to imagine a thievery so serious that it required payment in eternal currencies. He loved other songs more. A red valley by a red river. A boat owner named Michael rowing to a faraway shore. Knick-knacks, like his grandmother's green glass birds, the Paddywhacks, like his Irish ancestors, the giving of a bone to a dog. Still, the request for a home on top of an oven, the floorboards scorching your feet, then turning to ash? This was difficult to listen to. But the sight of tears being cheered up enough to go out and play with antelopes? What a powerful back yard to play in. What a wonderful, though ultimately homeless place to be.

Then In The Neighborhood Of Love

As a couple, they were a syntax of the wrong words in the wrong order. Their days had become a book of statements bound to emphasize their exhaustion with one another. Every phrase was punctuated by an ellipsis of silence. Big Love, which they believed would be the subject of the rest of their lives, barely lasted two years; but the divorce took another ten. By then they had mastered the domestic violence of being mutually present and mutually absent in the same room at the same time. By then, "love" was an independent clause they whispered in places beyond the radius of their rings and their doorbell. Then there was a sign. Then there was a truck. Then, they were gone.

PART II

Desire Never Gets A Snow Day

Desire never gets a snow day.
It bundles you up
And shovels the driveway.

Even warms up the car for you.

—

In eighth grade I whispered to the girl
Seated in front of me: "What did the telephone
Operator say to the fisherman?" She shrugged.

"I have salmon on the line."

—

Outside the ER doors
The voices of smokers
Push through a grey cloud of tobacco.

Inside, people are waiting to tell them something.

—

A man (near your age) reads his emails harshly.
He wants something he doesn't see there.
He worries it's not a mistake, or an oversight.

He feels foolish. But keeps reading.

—

If happiness is a cheering crowd,
Then desire is the empty seat belonging
To someone still driving around outside

Looking for a place to park.

Lunch With Michael Cohen In Prague

I hear #Prague #CzechRepublic is beautiful in the summertime.
I wouldn't know as I have never been.
-Michael Cohen tweet, 12-27-18

At a small white table
outside the eighth Starbucks
built in Prague

Michael Cohen squints,
looking up at the time
machine across the street—

a medieval astronomical clock,
the Orloj, with its figure of death
surrounded by the apostles

sounding the hours
and warning all to watch the stars
and mind their time

———

Time for lunch…

———

August in Prague. The height
of tourist season. American and Japanese
travelers mill down from Prague Castle

to the square, where the air
is a fusion of kolaches and coffee,
and voices grown loud with Pilsner

It is a good place
to see, without being seen
to speak, without being heard
On a napkin under a saucer
a man has written his own name
and under his name
he has written another

———

I was never there...

Pushing Shopping Carts Around What's Left

So now we cross each other's path
Pushing carts
Around what's left

Looking up at each other
Through puddles
Of almost clarity

The game of "Remember when…"
Played in shopping aisles
Of narrowing years

Was it you who told me
To accept that grief
Stains like a tattoo?

Remember when big fat Hope fell off a ladder?
Remember when "It could happen…"
Crashed into us?

Whenever I can't really remember
I lie, and say I do….
Because it changes nothing

Puddles pick up sunlight for a moment
Then clouds and murk return
Because nothing changes anymore

But the store stays open

Discernment

In the morning I lay out versions of myself.
I put them on the bed, and drape them
over a chair. I pace back and forth, or
I sit on the floor drinking tea
and staring at the choices.

Sometimes it's hard to separate a prayer
from a wish, a belief from the weariness
of asking more questions. Mornings can
break your resolve. You say "where do
I sign?" But a poem says "don't you dare!"

I live on the shore of a Great Lake.
41.4993° N, 81.6944° W. On the other shore,
42 miles due north, everything is the same.
Even Daylight Savings Time. It's hard to see,
but that's me waving to me from Canada.

At the autopsy of the star, the gallery
was filled with eager listeners. "A collision
with ideas, is noted. There's some concept
scarring. But a constant loss of light
through wormholes was the cause of death."

In the morning I separate the night from
from my other thoughts. It's like laundry.
I don't want the darkness to bleed through
the brightness. But it happens. So I'm off
to work like that—hoping no one notices.

Before You Said

Before you said what you said, before you took off your headphones and finished a text to the text before, before you agreed with the angle of your hair, changed your blouse, then changed back to the first blouse, before you asked me if I thought it would snow through the night, before you imagined I was having an affair with a woman who waived at me coming out of the library, and the one who lingered too long at our table in that restaurant that only takes cash, before you preferred blue skies to midwestern winters, before you said you were just making that up about the affairs, and hating your hair, before I made all of this up waiting for you to get ready to go to dinner, you said, "I'm not up for going out tonight. You?"

Questionnaire

If a poem falls off my desk, and is trampled on
By the cat, and scuffed by the bottom of the baby's diaper,

And sticks to the shoe of a policeman,
And tumbles a block in the wind,

Where it's sucked through the front door

Of the company you work for
As the cleaning crew leaves at midnight,

And is picked up by the night security guard
Who puts it in the break room by the donuts,

Where someone who thinks you like
"that kind of stuff" puts it on your desk

And you wad it up, unread, and throw it
Into a wastepaper basket,

Is it still a poem?
I don't know…

If you go to work and do
Just about nothing day after day

But still get paid, year after year,
Did you really go to work?

Seven Moon Poems

1

On a warm night the wind will
push lake breeze through the
the windows of an empty car.
The moon will see things differently.

2

There's the life we live,
the life we want, and the life
we will regret. The moon takes
notes. The moon keeps count.

3

The moon witnesses crimes
the sun will never see. It speaks
every dialect of fear, knows
and numbers every dark urge.

4

Summer. Waves touch the sand
of a public beach. Summer wind
cuts through layers of body heat.
The moon glowers at hidden figures.

5

We worship the sun, but welcome the moon.
One says "soon," the other says "now!"
One radiates. The other insinuates.
One looks down. The other looks around.

6

The moon is the nosiest neighbor
you will ever have. Keep your wits
about you. There's no such thing
as a moonless night. Close the blinds.

7

Some say the moon was struck and
half-blinded by cosmic debris. Perhaps so.
But the moon can hear better than
the sun. That's why we turn on music.

That's why we whisper.

Please Don't Hum

Please don't hum
Or tell me about another poem
That's "really great" while reading this

Don't visualize me on the other side of this paper

Standing in my kitchen
Hearing the cat crunch his food in the corner
While you read out loud

Please, just this once,
Let us quietly fall in love forever
With the same person

Communion

1.
Silence hugged and squeezed itself
Until a word was born, and another, and another
Until something that formed in one invisibility,
Fell into another...

2.
It's hard to separate the swimmer from the water
What with the immersion and the squeezing
From inside out and outside in—
And each wanting to be the one that goes,
And the one that stays

3.
And the runner? What about the runner?
The runner and the invisibility of air define each other—
The runner interrupting the air,
The air letting the runner run on

4.
Silence hugged and squeezed itself
Until a word was born, and another, and another
Until something that formed in one invisibility,
Fell into another...

5.
Even with shared lanes and false flips,
Wandering trails and slippery footing,
Sometimes the words still fall down inside you—

And when they do, it tastes like communion

The Lost Key To The Grateful Room

The news was whispered like subsonic alarms—
"The key to the Grateful Room can't be found.
People are trapped in there!"

Coming off a retreat some months before,
"The Power Of Thank You" plan was introduced.
Office procedures and company chemistry changed.

Hugs were suddenly everywhere. Tears, too.
The halls became so clogged with gratitude,
That large copy machines couldn't be delivered.

Weekly planning and accountability meetings
Became seats of confessions and awards of
Applause. Singular honors were unbundled.

The Break Room was eliminated.
The Grateful Room was added.
Then its one and only key was lost…

Desks were probed. Pockets were turned
Inside out. Lunch bags were torn open.
The phone rang. Even customers searched.

Still no key was found and little work was getting done.
Former feelings of value and appreciation dissipated.
The weight of relentless inconsequence bore down.

One locksmith came and failed. Another was angry.
"What's in there anyways?" "Can't you just do your
Business, wash your hands, and walk away?"

The CEO sent a memorandum to the shareholders:
The line of those needing a personalized thank you grows and grows.
The large bowls of self-applied-stick-on-kudos are going untouched.

I don't know what to do.

Lips Closed

In memory of M (1953 - 2002)

1.

The summer of 1975, our bodies
The temperature of warm green waves

In a Great Lake
Where our lips closed in on joy

(there's no other
word for it)

Later the moon and stars
Would come with drinks

To the island's Tiki bar
And light our wobbly walk

Back to that cottage with the breadbox
That said "EASY GREASY"

2.

We mimed the rest of that night
About the nature of love and absence

(of forgetting,
and the forgotten)

We didn't use words for what we said
Because no one can remember the future

But on the ferry back to the mainland
You made a gesture that had only one meaning:
You would always be living in my head

3.

What happened was going to happen
Other places, other lives, then a slow entombing death

But I didn't disappear the way you thought
I didn't vanish over decades of other summers

I was gone that night in the cottage
The moment the silence was so pure

I could hear fear
Talking behind my back

And calling me by my name

4.

You were right...
Your absence is always in me

Leaving my lips closed
And miming regrets

That no one but you can see

When You Didn't Respond

When you didn't respond to my
thoughtful emails, I received a batch
you didn't know you had sent. A sadness
with the same address as yours
was there, every time I checked.

———

Your voice once changed my life.
It was air that let me swim to the surface.
To sunlight and more air. Air to say thank you
for your perpetual joy.

———

Then time and thoughts changed your breathing.
Boredom shortened your sentences. I became
someone who made the mistake of wanting
to be loved out loud—the usual flaw
of putting desire into nearby words.

———

If I know what you will not say, who then is speaking?
If we both know what we won't say out loud,
are we still speaking? I only ask, because your voice
once changed my life. But nothing like this silence.

The Bottom of IT

Whatever IT is,
We don't really want to know.
But we like to think we do.

We like to go all shiny and confident
Promising to dive down
And get to the bottom of IT

But our lungs burn up.
Our brain floffles. We run out of air.
We panic.

Fear races us back to the surface of things.
Where we gulp down warm oxygen
And inhale the smell of offices and second homes.

Definitions and secrets,
Bafflements and old recordings
Of people who said they loved you

Litter the bottom of IT.

Letters you sent.
Letters you received. That day in 5th grade.
What really happened.

It's all there on the bottom.
Waiting. Waiting. Waiting
For your return.

This Poem Differently

You could write this poem differently
you could say the lines go like this:
sing me song loud (boom!)
let tea set go, pick up broom, race
to hide bong. Night now
is the hamster in your pillow case,
and the lawn hates your face. With
this poem, you will understand again
why car tires smell better than rakes, peonies
poplars, retractable pens, and the baby's playpen...
See what you did there?

Lost

I have nothing that cannot be lost
And I'm grateful

Not a coat, or a word, or how
I feel about you reading this

Or skipping over it…

Why do we want to keep ourselves
To ourselves so much?

What's lost was never loved
The way we said it was

That's why we lose it—
That's how it leaves us

Even here, where I talk about
Things that never happened

Where you get lost, and I
Come looking for you

All Day Cows

All day,
cows ruminate

and inundate
the blue sky

around an airfield

until all planes
are grounded...

waiting for darkness,
surrounded

by large fuel tanks
leaking methane

The Permissions Company

Permissions research and negotiation can make you want to tear your hair out.
The Permissions Company, Inc.

The line formed early and lasted
Until the doors were locked for the day
Some had faces on the verge of turning
Into clouds, others had hands disfigured
By years of prayerful supplication
Some had knees turned to mush
From decades of obeisance

Some carried empty bags,
Others, photos of people
They wanted to love
Some carried books filled
With things they wanted to say

Inside, some saw their mother, some
Their father, with a strange look on
Their face; in a conference room
Some saw former teachers and bosses
Seated at tiny desks, staring at a
Blackboard where it was written
Always ask for permission first

They had that same look

Anniversary In Dallas

Remember how wet
It was that day?

Those over-sized raindrops
Puckering the dust on our walk?

Remember how we stood
At the window, watching

The Trinity River
Flashing up, pretending

To be the Mississippi
Or the Ohio?

You and I own the right
To forget everything—

But I know you remember...

The wine that we chose
To have and to hold

Our drowning

After we lost hold
Of the unspoken inside us

Snorkeling Through City Lights, San Francisco

We were through with disappointment
Through with retro-new incomplete phases
With history turned into flavors of ice cream

Our fingers smelled like patchouli
Our hair like burning leaves
And cedar closets

It was the Saturday after that Monday
Or the Thursday before that Friday
Or maybe I'm forgetting on purpose

We snorkeled the Bakelite shelves
Of City Lights Bookstore, with our berets
Biker jackets, and half gallons of Chablis

We were darkness and burlesque
Going undercover under the covers—
Our eyes flashing inside masques

Down aisles of escape, and monuments
to monuments. We dove deeper and deeper
Until we lost sight of each other completely

I panicked and swam back to the door
Where I found Ferlinghetti floating
Face up, inches above the sidewalk—

He was pointing to a cluster of streetlights
In the rain, he was smiling and waving
I was just trying to catch my breath

Implanting The Appendix
Of Understanding

After the operation, things seemed
to make more sense. A clarity warmed
his body, feelings of confusion and
doubt seemed to have disappeared.

Greta Garbo's real last name
was "Garbanzo" (see legumes)
This is why she said "I want
be alone." It makes perfect
sense. It's not true; but sometimes
understanding works that way.

The ending is the ending.
No matter how many times you
push the "Up" button and say
things under your breath.
In the end, the elevator will not
change its mind or direction.

The three basic needs are food,
shelter and coupons clipped from
the smiles and laughter of those
you love. They're good for as
long as you live.

One night, a man woke up three
times. Each time, he tried to restart
his dream. Each time he failed.
That's when he understood:
There's more dream than time.

After the operation, things seemed
to make more sense. A clarity warmed

his body, feelings of confusion and
doubt seemed to have disappeared.

And There You Are

When we're a little old, we say
"back in the day" When we're
a little older than that, we say
"back when" Now we're really
old and we have nothing to say.

———

There's the time being, and being on time.
There's being and time. There's even
being and nothingness. Pick one and
stick with it for as long as you can.

———

Call me. You never will, and I won't
be waiting. But it's something to say
since we've broken our silence.
And we all know: you break something,
you have to pay for it.

———

I know you read the letters I wrote
to others while I slept. I know you forged
notes in the margins of my books
and tried to make them look like mine.
I know you want to know what I'm
thinking right now—and I know
you want to change it.

———

Call me. We will luxuriate in wonder.
Your name will appear on all my devices
at the same time. I have notes, the words
will work hard, I will too. Call me.

———

Black holes create gravity. Black holes
merge. They find each other. But we
don't know where they came from.
Are they where all the wrong thoughts
in history go?

———

You said it's not funny. It's not the time
for jokes. I only said "Here we are in the course
of human events, and in bad moods. How
long, Lord? How long?"

———

Heisenberg said things change while
being observed. Have I? Have you?
Are we still leaping low hurdles, and calling
them quantum leaps? People are talking.

———

If the past is a moving present, time
is out of mind, really. We don't lose
it or gain it. Something is nothing
and nothing is something. In the
timeless zone, will we even want to
see the ones we said we loved?

———

What are you driving at? What are you saying?
I'm saying we are all distracted drivers
and the engine keeps going long after
we shut the vehicle off. We take our eyes
off the road and hit a tree, we close our
eyes forever and we're still looky-loos.

———

What if this universe is just a dishrag
left on a sticky counter? Not a Luminous
or Sorrowful Mystery, but just a word
we use to make Sundays into theater
and weekdays more manageable.

———

We defy each other with our gratitude.
Each act a new art. Creations are born
out of "thou shall nots". It's all in the risk.
Be grateful for your fear, it makes
your chains clearly visible. The chains
you will break to make love and art.

———

I left you a voicemail: "I'm tired. I'm losing
interest. I'm not very good at finding things.
I know it's the middle of the night, but
call me." You didn't hear that. You probably
didn't read this either.

———

Live long enough, and what they call
"contemporary" will become "modern"
and what they call "modern" will become
"classic" and then it starts all over
again. Though post-modern is a new
amusement. But we don't forget our past;
it's how we pretend there's a future.

———

I turn out a light. But it continues through
the walls and the trees outside. No switch
can stop it now. I stare at the wall, where the
clock hangs. It's used to the stares of people
like me. We treat clocks like models and
celebrities, we look and see what we need
to see. I close my eyes. And there you are.

The Poetry Pogrom

I came to our pounded
Broken door wrinkled with sleep

They pushed past us, and began
Pulling books from shelves

They wore masks and smelled
Like bleach and road tar

They wore armbands
Depicting Pegasus crashing

Into a ranch-style home
And a steepled church

I was told to sit
My wife was told to stand

Over and over

"Stand up, one, two, Sit down,
Three, four, Stand up, one, two
Sit down, three four, Stand up,
Sit down…THREE-FOUR"

They powered-up laptops
And desktops, grabbed
Phones and notebooks

They knew all our passwords

My wife denied helping me—
It was our plan. She disappeared.

I am writing this from
An undisclosed location

If you can read this
I am no more

It is up to you now

Today's Date Minus 100 Years

(in memory of my father, an amputee, Timothy Edmund Donohue, 1907-1991)

On a Saturday 100 years ago
My father wakes up in his home,
his father already at work.

It's August 1919, in a town
Slightly west of Cleveland, Ohio.
My father is eleven, almost twelve…

His father, 43, superintends maintenance
of railway cars for a steel company.
In 18 years, it will be the Saturday

Of my father's Bachelor Party
After a day's work for his father
Surrounded by railroad wheels…

On that Saturday in 1919, I went to
A baseball game between Cleveland
And Boston with my best buddy,
Marcus "Punchy Cotton" Woolen

We had nickels for the streetcar
To League Park, and quarters for
Bleacher seats behind our heroes
Tris Speaker, centerfielder for Cleveland

And Babe Ruth, playing center for Boston.
It was a perfect day for baseball—warm air
And a blue cloudless sky. As usual, the
game began with a local talent singing

"Beautiful Ohio" like it was an opera—
I always rolled my eyes, to make "Punchy" laugh.

72

But the game was good. Really good, until…

Up 7-4 in the ninth, the Cleveland pitcher
got two outs, but loaded the bases. Then the
wrong reliever came in, to face Ruth.

His first pitch landed outside the park.
Grand slam. Boston 8, Cleveland 7—
The manager was fired after the game…

We didn't say much on the way home.
I thought it was the worst Saturday ever.
But I was wrong; as I'm sure you can imagine.

A View Resurrected

A tree blights up
and dies. A view is resurrected.
We return to what we forgot
we could see.

Laughter. It's the rain
you've been waiting for.
Now you can get through
this funeral, and the next.

There were moments
on the verge of perfect.
Fusion. Perception.
Compassion. Then fear
pulled up, honking its horn.

After the diagnosis
she turned pages slowly,
knowing a completion,
an absence is coming.

When the prettiest girl
in High School outlived
her beauty, the school
closed forever.

We start out being too
strong and too proud
to ask for help. We end
up on Facebook, aching
for prayers.

A tree blights up
and dies. A view is resurrected.

We return to what we forgot
we could see.

Different Meanings

The stagecoach arrived late.
Dusty from elsewhere. The actors
Mused where that was. Then
Began to rehearse.

Some say argument discovers truth.
Others say it buries truth the way
A photograph buries a painting
Of a photograph.

Each day I drive by a Day Care Center.
You know what they look like: plastic
Things in primary colors; children
Without a care in the world.

A farmer in a huge machine is laughing.
He waves at us as we stare. Bales of
Hay flopping in another large machine.
Later, horses consume his joy.

In England, five women wore large
hats a play we finally got tickets to.
I whispered to one, "The hats. Really?"
"I don't take your meaning," she said.

The End Of The Movement

The traffic slowed then stopped.
The cars and trucks froze as if
on a screen. No one could be
added or deleted. The program
for getting home would not respond.

———

You slowed, then stopped for
a photo I still have. You're
squinting at something we can
not see, your hand to your ear
as if you can't hear me, or
you're listening to years that
we haven't lived yet.

———

My mother's heart slowed then stopped.
Her blood's great work, was finished.
The light in her eyes flickered,
then fixed on the ceiling, as
the doors to her heart closed.

———

On the wall, a still life someone's father
brought home from the last French
gallery left in Da Nang. A half-loaf of
bread by a cracked vase with yellow
snapdragons. A thick lacquer applied
to keep the colors in place.

Dark Matter

The bigger meeting was off. The presentation was a bust. The fix was in. The play was pooched. "Creativity," I said. "Creativity is out of the question," you said. "Can't you realize we're on the edge of nothingness; heading towards Dark Matter that can swallow up agencies like ours in one gulp?" Outside, the mid-October sun lit up and lit down a blue-gray sky. Inside, we headed to elevators carrying portfolios with "Do Not Bend" tags attached to the handles. Farther away, we pictured the fire maples that ringed the yards of our homes. "Dark Matter," you said again. "Creativity," I said to myself.

Warm Bricks And A Quick Disguise

The word in prose is stone hard. The word in a poem is like a brick that maintains a fiery core that's curing forever. Poem-words are always becoming something else. Prose words are always repeating themselves. Prose goes after meaning like a fugitive task force. It captures everything it sees. It captivates the reader. But poetry is always on the lam, even when hiding in plain sight. Just yesterday, I saw a poem stop, turn its coat inside out, and walk right past a closely following reader. So it goes.

Uniforms

Could be the habit of a nun, or a man selling Whole Life
Coverage in a striped tie. Could be the black shirt and pants
tumbling in your dryer as you read this. Uniforms illuminate
us when our world goes dark. And who doesn't like a life that
comes with subtitles? Darkness surrounds us. We all want to
draw a tight circle around our fears. The pressed gray suit or a
muscular plaid for The Job. The Off The Rack Marriage with
guaranteed lifetime alterations. Anyone can cloister their life
in plain sight.

The Lecture

The learning begins when the door is closed. The first lesson is always about separating yourself from the thoughts and goals of others. The second lesson is Big Philosophy. It's about existence and non-existence. In the lecture room, the great questions simplify: you're either yourself or you're no one. Something or nothing. Present or absent. Someone calls your name, like God calling out to Abraham. You answer. Or you don't. You're ready or you're not. It's a lot to learn. And the lecture hasn't even begun.

The Tale Of The Dogs

Once there was a boy who grew up surrounded by Queens, New York. His name was Dom. Large for his age, he often acted the bully. He was a mediocre student. And unlike most boys in his neighborhood, he didn't have to cut lawns or shovel snow to have money for things like candy, or movie tickets, or presents for his family at Christmas. His father, Ted, gave him a generous allowance each Friday morning at breakfast. Always with the same words, "I'm so proud of you, my son." Other boys were jealous, but didn't say anything to his face. There was only one thing his father required him to do, and that was to feed two dogs that lived in the courtyard of an apartment building he owned a few blocks from their home. The dogs were left by a tenant who moved out shortly after the rents were raised twice in the same year. The father took over the vacated space as an office for himself. He had a secretary stock the office with dog food. But because the office was erratically used, he required his son to be sure the courtyard animals didn't go hungry. There was nothing unique about either animal. And it was never clear why Dom's father assumed the feeding of these abandoned dogs. They were unexceptional mixed breeds. The only real distinguishing difference was their temperaments. One was affable, and ready to play when Dom arrived to feed them. The other was always defensive and aggressive, barely trusting the boy, even though he was arriving with food. Once he snapped and lightly bruised the arm of the boy. Although angered, the boy actually admired the dog for his attitude. He liked the way the dog consistently snapped and growled. It made him cautious, but respectful. Months passed and the boy began to resent having to perform this one chore. There were new things to enjoy. Spring arrived. Sports, and girls occupied his mind. He complained to his father. His father wouldn't listen. "It's all I ask of you," he would say. The boy seethed in silence, then devised a solution. It was simple. He would feed only one of the dogs when he arrived. And when the unfed one died of hunger, he would arrange for the remaining dog to escape "by accident." He fed the mean dog. And eventually the other dog, wobbly with hunger, tried to eat from the mean dog's bowl. This triggered a violent attack, that resulted in the weakened, good natured animal dying from severe head and neck wounds. When the boy discovered the carcass the following day, he set the courtyard gate ajar, and unleashed the other dog. Then he quickly hauled the dead animal to a garbage can near the gate. He told his father that someone abducted the dogs, and expressed his anger and sadness in repeated phrases. And feeling suddenly grown up, he vowed to find "the kind of people who would do this." The father comforted him, and thanked him for his diligence. Later he laid down the evening paper, and reflected for more than a moment on how lucky he was to have such a son, for a son. And the boy up in his room, drawing a lewd sketch while pretending to do homework, laid down his pen for a moment, and thought the same. And just about then, the dog, unsure of his new-found surroundings, chased a pigeon into a busy street, where he was promptly hit and killed by a car that never stopped.

PART III

I Never Woke Up

What you want you will dream—
the life of your neighbor parked in your garage
the blossoms of poppies floating up your arm
and into your head

Driving with hands you can't see,
steering with your eyes, turning on green
and finding your mother in the kitchen
waiting to be fed…

That way you look over your shoulder,
your dark glasses, your confidence in
wakefulness—it's a retelling of how easy
wanting is confused with needing

In a dream something needed me
to stop wanting something it would
not name or point to, and I dreamt

I never woke up.

Light Blue Advertising Agency

The pounding in the head
From the night before
And the client meeting before that

The lost count of scotch and sodas
Missing from the song by the Kingston Trio
And found in the frown on a waitress's face

The boasts about showing the best ads
Known to man—but knowing that mankind
Had almost no desire to read or listen

The never forgetting that what we wanted
Could only happen if a certain "they"
Deigned to voice a certain "yes"…

Still, back at the advertising agency
We loved every minute of our
Near-art, pre-post-modern lives

Each morning being a re-creation of ourselves
From the starting point. Each piece
Renewing its part of the energy

Flowing through floors of polymaths
Breathing in the percussed air of
A non-digitized time on earth

And exhaled in the best works of
Our light-blue, carbon-dated lives

The Desired

The cake, the soufflé, the salmon.
The yellow dress, the antique bed, the view of Paris.
The lanky tour guide, the small museum, the translator
Studying for her medical license.
The croissants with jelly, the five photos
Taken by three women and two men.
The departure from the hotel
The flight home, the shower
We shared before unpacking.
As usual, it's only desire
That leaves so much
To be desired.

To Keep Us Silent

In the beginning there was noise
And it was good. We knew the seashore

From the sound of a palm tree in the wind,
Thunder, from the sound of feet

Stealing our goats. We gave all this vibrating
Air a name, and pursued all the sounds we found

In stones and sticks and bowls and
Hollow reeds.... Until campfires

Turned into conservatories,
And great halls were built

To keep us silent,
And listening

Just to them

Ship In A Bottle

Under the dark and darkening
Skies of bars

We sailed away from every reason
To jump ship, to port, to just be the life

That lived under our own eyelids…

We always drank till the money ran out
And always imagined ourselves into others;

Sometimes we were even right.

But when the third sheet's in the wind
You can't come about by reason.

You can't make any headway
Holding on to a dark bottle

Filled with dark waves
That promise to let you live

All your lives, all at once,
In that darkness

What Once Was Home

December, Ohio
Driving south by southwest
Wet snow falling and year round warnings
About bridges icing over
Before roads

On my way to what once was home
To see my daughter and grandsons
Living in the house
Her mother and I built
In the fall and winter of 1979

Long stretches of silence
Broken by me speaking to me
But in the voices of my dead father
And my dead brother:

Did you do this, did you
Do that, fix that, find this,
Don't hahaha me, I'll bet
You forgot to change
Add, replace, rotate, clean…

It goes on for miles and miles
As usual, I am never really alone

Then just past Texarkana
I pull over to check the map
Near a roadside billboard. As I pull away
Its message appears in my rearview mirror :
Scenic Overlook Ahead
Closed For Repairs

We all laugh, but no one says another word

Mark Strand's Guitar

Mark Strand's guitar (the Strandsky)
Was made on Prince Edward Island, Canada, in 1934

It traveled to Yellow Springs, Ohio,
New Haven, Connecticut
Iowa City, Iowa

And finally, New York City
Where it was stolen,
On the night of November 29, 2014

Pre-tuned to the key of absences
The guitar was never seen again
But luckily, we have recordings

Birthday Bash At Horace's Place, December 8, 18 BC

"prodesse et delectare" -Horace

Shortly before his 46th birthday
party, on a cool day in Rome 2,037
years ago, Horace, named Quintas
Haratius Flaccus by his parents,
sampled a new wine from Verona.
It was light and semi-sweet, and
would surprise his birthday guests.
As usual Horace wrote about his
life and times in hexameter lines
as his sons wrestled and his daughter
practiced the lyre. And as usual he
pondered why he bothered to
write poems or recall certain
moments, day after day...
His hijinks with Cicero Minor,
his constant interrupting of his
teachers in Rome and Athens,
My embarrassment at losing my
shield and running backwards
at the Battle of Philippi...
But there wasn't time for
that now—guests would be
arriving soon. So he made
a note that said *see shame,*
then quickly wrote *poems*
should delight and instruct...

Frozen Fire Losses

After the fires of regret
Burned through the floors
Of our anger and blame

We fell into matching isolations.

The memory of certain
Words melted the weld
Between us, and we became

Two halves of the same possibility.

On the day of the fire
We talked face-to-face,
Leaning into a rearview mirror.

You in the back seat.
Me driving way too fast.
Before we were finished

Your words were incarnated
In my head. And mine, in yours.
It was a bitter communion.

It took years, but we finally
Learned that what is frozen
Can burn like fire. Loss is loss.

Today you live where things
Fell apart between us.
You've done a lot with the place.

Some things are still hot to the touch;
But it's just the Texas summer, and
Two halves of the same possibility.

Orient-R

We three kings
of Orient

Are

Looking for
a comma.

We R-not
a chemical element

Nor are we
"No such address"

Will trade
one or more kingdoms

For a comma
we can hear

In mid-air.

Contact manger,
Bethlehem

What We Do Later

We squeeze out a few more words that surprise us
And make the ones we love laugh

We eat a bowl of ice cream without regrets, choking, or
cardiac arrest

We see a film we slept through on a date in the 1970's
And say "I remember it all like it was yesterday!"...

At least ten times a day
Death thinks about us

And we think back

Not Another Poem About Death

for my daughter

It's not another poem about death
when I remember your voice
or your smile …

———

All the good pictures are already taken.
I just aim the piano
and there you are.

———

So the notes go down, when they should go up.
Alright. OK. Either way, the intonations detonate
serial silences, and there you are again…

———

I was planning to tell you a different story from the
beginning.

———

In a crematorium, a young assistant
follows instructions to put a wooden clock
inside the cardboard body-box

In the words of the deceased
"I burned through all the time I had.
Be sure a clock goes with me"

———

It's a $79.99 up-charge—if you're interested.

———

All good poems aren't already written. *And they're not dead.*
You just have to hear them in the keyboard.

———

A few months later, according to his wishes,
the family took the ashes of his body and the ashes of a clock
to the end of a pier in a lake near his boyhood home

The lake that passed through his bedroom screens
with fecund green breezes before rainfall
and sultry gusts before thunder

———

He never doubted his sure-footed stance
on what word said how many times
would suffocate a poem or love

"The loss of time made his last years
ambidextrous. He learned to use
both sides of a clock," said a friend

———

Still, others want to know
how this poem *that's not about death*
will meet its own ending.

———

I know *you* already know.
But read it again. I'll read it with you.
We'll have a laugh…

Green Jeep, Red Light

It was so long ago
And she is so young (I think)
It might have been her great grandfather

Maybe great-great grandfather
Who first drove a Jeep like that
Through bullets and mud

Far away from this sunny day
Smelling like summer grass
And suntan lotion

Today the girl presses what's left (there are no doors)
Of an ancient green war machine
Back into service

Her patrol, a small lakefront town
Her commission, to lead a platoon of new recruits
Into conflicts of erotic confusion and courage

She, in her uniform of summer tan
And wearing a yellow two piece,
And helmet of shiny blond hair…

Bathed in the decibels of her sound system
I idle behind her, waiting for the light to change
Watching as she forms a gun with her thumb and index finger

That she smilingly aims at a boy
Staring non-stop at her
From the curb of a crosswalk…

When the light changes,
Everything changes:

When I count to three

You will forget everything

Except something
About the forever
Birth of desire

After June 22, 1971

("Blue" by Joni Mitchell, Warner Brothers Records, Inc., 1971)

After the Beatles
We all played in a band
In our head

Pretending to be all that we heard
About needing nothing
But love

We played joy loud
With friends
In dorms

And little bars
After summer jobs
That mercifully ended

In long drives back to school...

But then came "Blue"
And words like "love"
Would form a bumpy rash

Of braille
In our throats

After "Blue"
We began searching
The eyes of strangers

For one
Who could read
All the superimposed captions
Scrolling through our souls...

And still stay
And still say
"Here"

"Here is a song,
for you"

First You Must Find A Wooden Piano

First, you must find a wooden piano.
One that has no current to connect to
Other than you.

It must also have all 88 of its keys.

Now count to key 42, going from left
To right and push your right thumb
Down on that key:

This is the sound of letter "D"

Then put your index finger
Down on the adjacent key
The one called letter "E"

(on a map other than Google
you're now two towns
past Middle C)

While undulating
These two keys, extend your pinkie
Five keys to the right

And touch the sound of an "A"
Hmmmmmm. Hear that?
Try it more than once.

(To recap, thus far you have played D, E, A)

Finally, and resolutely
Fly the index finger of your left hand,

Landing it like a grackle

On yet another "D"

One that's five keys from "A"
And twelve away from that "D"
That's under your thumb...

But take your time
Take your time

Out Of Order

1.
You passed
You failed
Couldn't love you more

It's over

2.
With distinction We have to let you go
It's a girl!
I want to see other people

Please call me
Please don't do that
Hope to see you there

3.
This isn't working for me anymore Anything but poetry!

4.
I love the way you laugh It's not you it's me
I just can't
I will always

5.
Me too you
I'm going with "thrilled to death"
Maiden name? Timothy!

6.
The elevator is out of order
An inconvenience A poem will love you more
Hope to see you there

The Thread

The shirt falls down
The chairback
Where the cat
Leans forward
Inhaling
The resurrection
And the life
Of things
Forgotten

And hanging
By a thread

Mythology

What when
Were you expecting?

What now
Was that?

You like the word mythology
Because you think it's old and studied
But it's just a story of choices, like the menu
You read this morning at Don's Pancake Palace

That was you going all Homer-
On-Hector when you ordered the blintzes
With "lightly scrambled eggs on the side"
When you made the waitress listen

To how you stood up to that tire dealer
How you made him yield and surrender
A two-tire discount and a free coffee
From the Starbucks across the street

Repeat it all to the family at supper
And tonight, when the room is all blackness
And the air smells heavy with dark water
And you're feeling all blind and unlettered

That's when the waitress will remember you
And when we will all understand how much
You desire pancakes, and tires at a discount
And stories about yourself

What when
Were you expecting?

What now
Was that?

Then He Spoke

For five years, my cat
opened his mouth and
nothing came out; he feared
his voice, would damage his voice.
I know. But it's true.

Then one day it happened :

Years of frustration poured
out of him. The sun in winter,
the thunder in summer, the
birds taunting him, window
by window in our home

"If only I could…"

Could what, Mr. Cat? Fly through
glass, and above the trees, following
the river to the lake, and the lake
to Canada, where you would
join a gaggle of Canadian geese?

You? You not understanding their
language? You, finally talking,
but having nothing to say because
no one can understand you when
you speak?

Let's start over.
What say you?

Branchless Trees

The cat lounges on a window sill, his tail
on auto-twitch. Inches away, starlings, grackles
and jays pass through rain-scented air,
unfazed by an enemy able to perch
in branchless trees.

The Man Six Stories Below Me

The man with cancer
Six stories below me
Walks an invisible dog

He stops and stares
At trees without leaves
On a corner without cars

Heavy flakes of snow
Fall from a late winter sky,
He looks up, without blinking

He doesn't see me
But I know he feels
Someone is watching him

I scan the sky
He looks down
The dog is long gone

After The Doctor's Office

After the doctor's office
vital aspects
are shared

in complex sentences
drawn up in a place
we will never see

containing blood
that never stops
shouting "thief!"

"thief!"

Waves Of Serenity

If time is a particle wave
That never accumulates, then there's really
Nothing to remember, and nothing to forget

Still, the idea of "one day at a time"
Sounds good. Makes sense. Just break living
Into particles too small to fear or regret

It's hard to resist a serenity like that—
Something-something between nothing and nothing
No big deals coming one way or another

Nothing appears out of order
No one takes the wrong train or exit
No one disappears ahead of time...

Wow. What French philosopher, or Irish
Aunt came up with that? "Everything
Is exactly as it should be," as you say

So tell me, what can we do about
12:00 PM EST, January 20, 2017?
Can it be broken into particles

So small, parts of it never happened?

Dark Matter (II)

Some say the heart of the universe is a black hole. Dark
matter at the edge of time and eternity. A ferocious
nothingness, sucking everything and everyone into forever
absence. But at the center of our little affection (I've tried to
say this before) was nothing but a cup of black coffee. That,
and my need to talk about the structure of Jobim's *Trem Azul*,
and Portuguese verbs. It was never lives of happiness at the
edge of darkness. It was always coffee, near the brim of a cup,
made with water from the River of Saudade.

Dinner At One Hand Clapping

So we journeyed to Sound, to dine at One Hand Clapping, the most famous restaurant in the world. The one with a menu without prices by entrees. It seemed like a cool and jokey idea. It was a long pleasurable evening of complex and simple flavors in entrees of contrasting textures and colors. We tasted things without names. Finally, the waiter arrived and presented us with the mysterious bill. We emptied our wallets and pockets but were informed that we were "short of the required amount." Unnerved and embarrassed (a sign written in seven languages said Local Currency Only) we presented traditional instruments of credit. These were called "useless" and were cut into pieces in front of us. We looked at each other and saw anger and fear. We accused each other of things that happened years ago. Then a serious, but smiling woman asked if we had anything else to "put on the table?" We conferred. Then shouted. Then stood up, and pulled wads of fear, anger and selfishness out of each other in a noisy, messy, flurry. We piled it all on our table. Waiters wearing special uniforms appeared, and took everything away on a giant glass trays. Then the woman returned, with a receipt. Shortly afterwards, the manager asked if he could get us anything else. Outside, the morning sky was layered with tones of peach and mango with hints of blood orange. It pressed against the windows of One Hand Clapping. No one made a sound.

The New Car Of Their Love

Their names? I don't remember their names. I barely remember their existence. He wore a black shirt. She wore off-brand purple yoga pants. And? And they talked their way out of the new car of their love, arguing over too many options. What did you say? That there's something to be said for a couple enjoying simple reliable transportation between now and the inevitable. What inevitable would that be? Separation. From each other? Yes. And? And everything else. You said that? Yes.

Lines Written By A Bass Player

You can't see anything if you look with your mouth. So the phone is silenced. I'm in the car, the sun is setting. It's Winter O' Clock. Snow is dusting the road and jumping up and around the tires in front of me. I'm thinking about the road turning colder and colder and wrapped in whiter and whiter sheets. I'm thinking about driving on a tiny corner of the earth's winding sheet. I'm thinking about gravity's great love for us all. Keeping us from flying off the round edges of the world. Keeping us grounded. I'm thinking how maybe gravity loves too much; forcing us to build bigger and bigger rockets to get away. To take a break somewhere gravity can't reach us. But today, like every day about now, I'm heading home from the gym to feed the cat and maybe make my wife laugh. Later I'll write a poem about the simple, tiny, perfect lines a bass player wrote and played in a famous song. Amazing. It's like a poem within a poem. I hope I can pull it off.

Upbeat Emails From The Poem Family

The poem doesn't mean to scare you. It just calls in the middle of the night because it knows that's when you'll be home. Unlike novels, a poem can blend in perfectly with the work papers on your desk, the work you're avoiding—the work they pay you for. That poem you lost when your car ran out of gas on the coldest night in Oklahoma history? It never held it against you. Stop fretting. Finally, as a book, poems know the other books will laugh at them. It doesn't care. You don't have to hide it by a bookend. Talk to you soon.

PART IV

The Third Professor Of The Day

The third professor of the day is always
the tiredest. But don't be discouraged.
The truest poetry is the most feigning.

When you read this, the first voice you hear
will be mine. Toward the end, it will be yours.
I'll be listening to you.

In every conflict, there's a point of no
return—whether it's a hostile takeover
or a tennis match.

In its fourth lunation, the moon will withdraw
its approval of you. Everything will change in
ways you can't put your finger on.

After the school, the job, the income beyond
most worries, you get grilled about
how you're spending your time.

When you say I'm not who you think
I am, I know you've been reading poems
I haven't seen yet.

Let's look on the bright side. Even if
there's glare and we have to squint. Even if
the lights turn out to be a tanning bed.

Close To Never Again

When you asked to see me
I wondered if I could take your place.
Something I said I would do

Should something like that find you,
Hiding (probably) under sheets
And trying not to laugh.

I meant what I said,
But that was way back when, and this,
This was closer to never again…

In the hospital room, you were gone.
I listened to words wrapped
In starched white coats

That rose above your bed
Like mountains of snow
You would never see again

But I returned in the spring
To see that view for myself
And be closer to never again.

My Own Mistakes

I trust your
mistakes, more
than my own.

It's not about
desire, or art
or love.

Yes, it is.

Conjunctions

Wired for more,
We're charged by the conjunctions
Of self and world

Son and father
Mr. and Mrs.
So and so, who's such and such—

The first thing we learn to do over
Is who we say we are.

The sinner becoming a saint
The apostle becoming an apostate
A hand becoming a fist

It all depends on how an ampersand
Can widen the pupils of our eyes
Fixed in this world around us

We may be X, Y and Z
Or (XX), (XY) and Z
But everything happens

In the conjunctions
Between ourselves
And everything else.

Sun and stars
Darkness and light
Land and water

Even The One
Who needed nothing
Wanted more

The Easiest Thing In The World

To say no
To stay put
To suppress yes

To not love
To not write
To not speak...

To become
The only one
Who sees you

Waving goodbye

To you
And you
And you

Every morning

Poem On Writing Poems

If you say you are writing
just for yourself, call everything
a beginning. It doesn't matter where
the ending takes you. But know
it will always get there ahead of you.

"Not ideas, but things." Yes. But things
doing things they weren't supposed
to do, is a better idea. Let the wheelbarrow
do a rain dance. Have a plum eat a poem.
Be the best hyphenated-poet you can be. *(1)*

What you remember
is the oldest and brightest blood
within you. When it comes
around, let it fill your heart
to the brim.

When nobody tells you
what your style is, thank them.
When no one says your work
reminds them of so and so
know you are free. Get busy.

Don't imitate the famous names. They were
as sure as you that their poems were (or
or will be) a fraud. Borrowing their voice
will only make you cough, and your
poems will look like half-eaten pastry.

Don't write poems to be read
after you're dead. Write poems to your
16-year-old self. Let her know how well
things worked out. Tell him
he was right. Enjoy the endings.

I know they pounded "Make it new"
into you. I know you are tired of carrying
that leather bag through empty, dusty
train stations. Don't. The saying wasn't
even new, it was Confucius. Make it up. *(2)*

If you expect someone to listen to your
poem, imagine more than their eyes and
ears. Respect the gift of their time, and
imagine the bad days they have endured.
It will help you get somewhere together.

For centuries, popular songs have had
an average length of two minutes and
twenty-six seconds. You can look that
up and listen for days. Start anywhere,
but start. Write to the poem's 2:26

Eve was stronger than Adam.
And braver. Eve wanted to know
what's what. Adam watched creation
and named animals. Eve found out
what creation tastes like. Be Eve. *(3)*

Optional Notes

(1) William Carlos Williams, "A Sort of Song" Poetry Magazine, 1914 and
Patterson Book I (1927) , "The Red Wheelbarrow" and "This Is Just To Say,"
in The Collected Poems of William Carlos Williams, Volume I (1938)
(2) Make It New Essays, Ezra Pound, (Faber & Faber), London, 1934, "In a
Station of the Metro," Poetry Magazine, (1913)
(3) Book of Genesis, Chapter 3

Experimental Phrases

More and more, what happened
so fast in our fewest days,
becomes "we'll see" as we age.

——

I think we need each other...
So we'll meet for drinks...
Have you ever kayaked?

——

You are either right or wrong.
Achieve or leave. Ask or not.
Experimental phrases mean risk.

——

I saw something in your X-rays...
You could fight this...
Two, maybe three months...

——

What begins with screamy-gasps
in one darkened room, starts
over in another: feelings then feedings...

——

Do you remember the cooing,
the vows of forever love whispered on
your pre-alphabetized bald head?

——

Beware: desire has a half-life of 1,000 years.
Experience will often fail here;
False positives abound.

——

Meanwhile, around the planet
another generation arrives,
mouths at the ready.

———

We'll see. *They'll see.*

The Patient

The patient denied his need for treatment
Denied he was a patient
Denied he was in a room
Frequented by patients

Outside, car horns and conversations
Floated in a mid-morning of a Tuesday

"We are here to help you,"
Said one of three masked man
"You've had quite a shock," said another
"How do you feel today," said the third

The patient felt his weight pushing against a mattress
The patient felt his heart pushing against his chest
Two heavy-set women wearing plum-colored smocks
Entered the room and busied themselves with machines

"Let the doctors help you hon," said the largest of the two

This infuriated the masked men, now holding scalpels
And wearing special reading glasses
They demanded that the room be cleared

Then the sound of someone sitting and rising was heard
Sitting and rising from a soft leather chair: siii, siii, siii
Then blackness and classical music heard through wooden
earmuffs

Outside, in a parked car, someone wearing dark glasses
Drinks milk from cows that live in trees
And waits, and waits, and waits...
Maybe it was a Wednesday

In Line At The UPS Store

In line at the UPS store
Something about something not packed
Something about time not being there
When most needed

‾‾‾‾‾

I read obits in a newspaper
Still made out of paper. Death notices
The old way. Ones that black-ink your fingers
With words of the end of time

‾‾‾‾‾

The line grows. A thrown-open package
Litters the counter and floor. A small face sobs.
A woman steps forward to comfort,
Her eyes, absorbing pain like blue towels

‾‾‾‾‾

Some pass away. Some go home.
One had a last wish: "Please don't vote for Trump!"
Cleveland Plain Dealer, October, 2016

‾‾‾‾‾

Blue towels to small face:
"It's bad, you're right, but it's not the end
of the world. No one died."

‾‾‾‾‾

There will be other boxes
Other containers, ready to ship
There will be oncoming traffic in the passing lane
There will be things you can't see your way around

‾‾‾‾‾

Meantime, there are other reasons to sob
And the line is backing up, and up and up

Sonnets

Sonnets are about sonnets
The way wood frames around art
Are about tree surgeons

Rather than art

Still we continue to chisel
Through marble credenza drawers
Hoping to find the cadenza

Hidden in this cenotaph
Of lyric poetry

Lexeme Dream

Joy is everywhere
And suffering is everywhere
But you and I cannot be
Everywhere at once

Here and there. Here. And there.

Do you remember what you said
When wonder moved boxes of anger
Out of the way, and cleaned off tables
Sticky with the past?

Now and then. Now. And then.

If you can hear me, tell me:
Is all this really just a hiccup of joy?
Is light always a complete sentence
Everywhere you walk over there?

My mother died in her sleep. Age 98.

Do you really die at all
If you die like that?
Or do you just wake up
Go to the bathroom
And start a new dream

Forever…

Wooden Desks

You raised your arms
above your head
and touched your fingers
forming an empty circle

"This is the loophole that none shall pass through"

It was larger than the eye of a needle
and smaller than a camel.
Some of us thought you
were referring to
the paperwork
of love

———

Back at the blackboard,
20 years before, a nun
in a nun's habit drew a circle
in pink chalk

"This is the hypocenter of an earthquake"

We imagined a deep rumble
coming up through the floor
from the school's steam-heat boiler room,
vibrating our pant legs, thighs and skirts
and rocking our wooden desks
with their holes for inkwells
that we didn't understand
and never used.

———

Years later, after the marriages
and divorces. After we
ratted each other out
behind the two-way mirrors
of parties and family reunions,
I still don't understand
that gesture : I was no lawyer
and you were no ballerina.

————

Did the nun know?

The Metronome And The Night Trees

Summer,
a line of trees
absorbing darkness

Inside

a piano
a metronome
a man in his sixties

———

The nature
of music
is the nature

of time itself

the measure
of motion
and change

of sound
counting
on sound

to appear
and disappear
according to plan

———

A man plays
a piece he's played
for years

Time-checked
by a metronome
set to *presto*

It doesn't take long :
seven measures in
the fingers collapse

The room goes silent
except for the
tsk, tsk, tsking

of the metronome

———

Summer,
the windows
are open,

no wind
moves the trees
in measured gusts,

the night
is exactly as
it should be

The moon
with its grey smudges
above the trees,

The trees
absorbing
the loss of light

139

and accepting
the stillness
that comes

from the absence
of breeze
touching

the fingers
of their limbs

Seven Window Poems

1
Try to remember what you see.
Old age removes memories
Before it removes your eyes.

2
The cold rain doesn't hate your hair.
The blizzard doesn't know about
Your doctor's appointment. Look again.

3
As you can see, frames
Help you focus on the middle.
Things you can't see, surround you.

4
Streams of sunlight. Warmth.
Transparency. Still, it's winter.
What an unclear truth February is.

5
A bird saw a way out
But the exit was something else.
It cost the bird its life.

6
What is seen, is believed.
What you recall, is hidden.
Faith is for your eyes only.

7
At night, the outside
Looks in at the illuminated life
You live. I only see the darkness.

In The Dark

I miss talking to you
So I take old conversations
Out of the giant freezer

And listen to our voices
Thawing out in a room
You've never seen

November 2, Near Lake Erie

November near Lake Erie,
The trees that sometimes minimize our northern views
Are almost out of leaves –
Distances are devoured by November
Occlusions are dissolved,
November 2, The Feast of All Souls –
The communion of absence and presence...

In November the northern land empties itself of itself,
But this great lake will stay green and deep forever –
Churning waves in the branches of bare trees,
And letting me walk a shoreline for months
Without moving from a window,
Or changing my address

The Conestoga Wagon Of Perfection

Perfection, with the possible exception of the first
Moon landing, is overweighted and over-rated.
Can anything be improved until it is faultless?
A divine mystery on earth? *The blue suit that*
Showed off her blond hair to perfection—
I am told she is perfection itself...

The Perfection Confection Store you pass each morning,
Sweet things waiting in trays, and the Santa-sized baker
Waving, motioning to you through the shop window
The satiny perfection of her skin, his pursuit of golfing perfection—
I am told she strove to be the perfect wife...

Perfection eats and sleeps under your pillow, and keeps
You awake. Perfection downsizes joy to a corner of your
Glove compartment, where it's locked up and forgotten
I am told she was perfect in French and Giles was perfect for her—
Ten years older and with his own career...

The Conestoga Wagon of Perfection, the bumpy ride
With you inside, always heading to where the light ends
I'm telling you it's OK to lose your way a little—
It's OK to arrive a little late, and laughing...

Second Thoughts

In any second-hand store
You can hear the voices that get left
In fabrics. The anguish of a shirt
On a trip to Greece, the talk between
Two winter coats about holidays.

In Manhattan, the Q train serves
Second Avenue from 96th Street
To 72nd Street. There's a Goodwill
Store at 88th and Second Avenue.
You won't believe what's said in there.

Look, since the last shall be first,
and the first shall be last, it's good
to be second in line. Count on
on things reversing themselves,
before you give up your place.

The Obituaried Inventory Of Likes

For Mary of Loudonville, age unknown,
It was golfing in Florida and her nieces

Robert, 52, born in Chicago, but reared in Newark
Enjoyed his dog Robix, and another named Whisper

Lotti, 91, of Fort Worth
Liked Blue Bell Ice Cream
The Mesquite Rodeo, and Gunsmoke

Because the living have no power over death
Because the dead have no say about the after of their life
Most obituaries leave a trail of questions:

What about that love of Nietzsche
That was burned out of Mary
By golf course sunlight?

What do we call the complex system of phenomenology
That Lotti discovered in the bottom of bowls--the one
That made her doubt the nature of ice and sugar?

And wouldn't it be refreshing
To know that Robert preferred to pretend
That Whisper was a woman that led him on a leash

Naked through Newark

The Comparative Nature of Names

for Dan and Virginia

Bob is no Phil
But wants to be Phil
Who is married to Paulette
Who knew Bob
Would never make much of himself

Paulette had a sense about such things
She was alternately loved and hated
By Priscilla who wished she could have shoes like Paulette
But let Paulette copy answers
From her geometry homework

A class Bob flunked
Almost twice

At their 10th reunion
Bob got Phil a drink at the open bar
But forgot Phil said
"Hold the ice!"
And as Bob returned to the bar
Priscilla and Paulette
Walked whispering
Through a door marked "Women"

In almost the same shoes

Tempestuous

"Shake it off..."
The Tempest, Act I, Scene 2

The major lyric poet before Shakespeare was?…
Thomas Wyatt. I forgot that. Perhaps you did too.
It also says *(here)* that Harvard University was founded
Twenty years after Shakespeare died; adding that
"Wyatt's was the name of a chain of cafeterias
founded in Texas in 1957."

———

Texas doesn't have a town named after Shakespeare.
Surprising, because it does have a town called Marfa,
named after (a) Marfa Ignatievna in Dostoevsky's
The Brothers Karamazov, or (b) Marfa Strogoff, a character
in Jules Verne's novel *Michael Strogoff.* Nobody's sure.

———

In Roman Catholic churches there are marble half-shells
filled with water blessed by a priest, that flank the
entrances to the nave. It's a special kind of cleaning fluid
for your right hand, the one used to make the sign of
the cross. It's not a secret sign anymore.

———

Thomas Wyatt introduced the Petrarchan sonnet
to the English-speaking world. But it took Shakespeare
to write really, really good ones. Oh, and his plays! Big
beautiful stagey poems. Still, it took centuries to get rid
of what became sonnet addictions, The ABBA-ABBA
dos and don'ts. The geegaws of rhyming.

———

Then there's the failed Roman Catholic, John Donne.
Though his mother was related to Thomas More,

he didn't want to die for being a Catholic, like his
brother, who deceased in jail for sheltering a priest.
Donne, who knew his way around a poem, stopped
attending mass, married cleverly, went to jail for doing
so, and wrote anti-Catholic pamphlets.

———

Jesus stopped the storm that frightened the men
on the Sea of Galilee. But no one could calm the Atlantic
tempest in 1609 that engulfed the *Sea Venture*. Its masts
shorn by gales, the ship was torn apart, beaching survivors
on an island of spells and ghosts; of sorcery, incantations,
and other magics: Bermuda.

———

In Roman Catholic churches, bread is tinctured with wine.
The body and blood of Christ is transubstantiated. The living
and the dead are in communion with the risen Christ, and one
another. A thurifer holds a thurible, as a priest puts incense
on coals, making the air fragrant with the sacred.

———

Time, which in itself is invisible, is in the cellar of words.
Down below the floors of consciousness, mixing things up.
Temptation. Temporary. Tempest. The name of a car made
by General Motors, Pontiac Division, between 1960 and 1970.
Then again from 1987 to 1991. Then never again.

———

In the early morning of Friday, October 21, 2016, I awoke
from a dream. In this dream, the phrase "Through the reigns
of heartfelt utopia" kept repeating itself. I got out of bed and
wrote it down. Reigns. Not reins. Or rains. It was exactly
4:30 AM. It was my 64th birthday.

———

Wyatt's cafeterias closed in 2003. General Motors declared
bankruptcy at approximately 8:00 AM on June 1, 2009.
It had $82 billion in assets and $172 billion in debts.
A financial tempest thundered for days and months.
Thousands of workers lost faith in promises and other
things unseen. The Pontiac Division was disemboweled.

―――

In 1608, John Donne wrote *Biathanatos*. A long way from
The Holy Sonnets, here the poet (now clergyman), sets out a
heterodox defense of self-homicide, of suicide. It comes
complete with examples: Sampson, Saul, Judas Iscariot,
and Jesus. "This will prick Death's pride," he thought.
"But I will decide when the bell shall toll for me."

―――

Shakespeare wanted to retire. He had a great roster
of money-makers but needed one more. So he wrote
The Tempest, his last play. He wanted out of London.
He wanted to spend time with his wife and grandchild
at New Place, the second largest home in Stratford…
And to purchase Blackfriars Gatehouse, which some
say was a safe house for priests and secret masses.

―――

On October 21, 2016, my 64th birthday,
Leonard Cohen released his final musical recording :
Darker. Seventeen days later he died in his sleep.
The following day, on November 8, 2016,
Donald Trump lost the popular vote 62,979,636
to 65,844,610—and became the 45th president.

Optional Notes

William Shakespeare (1564-1616)
The Tempest (most likely written 1610-1611)

Sir Thomas Wyatt (1503-1542) various sonnets

Motto of Harvard University in English, "Truth"

Wyatt's Cafeterias, founded, Dallas, Texas in 1957.
"Cuisine The Soul of Texas (Some Profound Thoughts
On The Cafeteria Life)," Skip Hollandsworth,
D Magazine, January, 1984

Francesco Petrarch (Petrarca) (1304 -1374)

For more on the Roman Catholic dogmas of
transubstantiation and communion, see *Canons of the
Fourth Lateran Council,* 1215. Notably, Canon 1 and
Article 3, "The Sacrament of the Eucharist,"
Catechism of the Catholic Church.

John Donne (1572-1631) *Death Be Not Proud,
No Man is an Island (Meditation XVII, Devotions upon
Emergent Occasions), Biathanatos* (1608) and various

*An Account of the Incidents, from which the Title and Part
of the Story of Shakespeare's Tempest were derived,
and its true date ascertained,* Edmond Malone, 1808

"1964 Pontiac Tempest GTO Tested,"
Car and Driver Magazine, January 1, 1970

GM History" in corporation's archive,
first filed May 2, 2009

Leonard Cohen (1934-2016). *You Want It Darker,*
Columbia/Sony Music, released October 21, 2016

*The Mueller Report (Presented With Related Material
By The Washington Post)* Introduction and Analysis

by Reporters Rosalind S. Helderman and Matt Zapotsky,
2019

See signed indenture of mortgage,
William Shakespeare, March 11, 1613
(British Library)

Our New Names

At that restaurant
when you were about
to speak

When the moment
was about to become
the matter between

our new names
of Plaintiff
and Respondent

I saw you again
studying in the library
100 years before

your beautiful mind
unaware of your
beautiful body

your eyes in a book
by an author who
wouldn't like you

because you could
finish his sentences
before he wrote them

which bored you
which made you
look up and smile

at me staring at you

A View From Above The Cleveland Yacht Club

From the mouth
Of Lake Erie, spring brings
Barges with yellow machines
Digging black holes
On the bottom
Of the Rocky River
To ensure that the keels
Of great-sailed boats
Can only be stalled
By white flares
From empty decks
In summer glare

The Lines Of Your Thinking

We followed the lines of your thinking,
And reached a snowy mountaintop.

We stepped over the remains of those who got there first
And found you drinking heavily in a sprawling shack of books.

We were hungry, and you did not feed us.
We were thirsty, and you did not offer us water.
We were cold, and you said "Hey, things happen…"

You gave us a box of books we had already read
And said, "Burn these for warmth
Then show yourselves out."

The Way Of Sorrows

The summer sun. July or August. Wind in the maple trees on
the tree lawns pushing warmth, like a low fi sound, down the
sidewalk and into the field next to my childhood home. An
acre of milkweed and hawthorn trees between our house and
the neighbor's. Two lots that didn't sell in 1926 when the
block was first built. By the fall of 1929, the families of
would-be neighbors would never arrive. Gone to look for
work in Cleveland, or back to Newark or Italy or Poland.
Summer, 1962. A field of milkweed and chicory blossoms
feeding monarch butterflies, and three hawthorn trees with
their canopies of limbs that you could slide under. Where I
would sit, invisible in its dark grotto of thorns like those used
to crown the head of Christ. There, in summer, under the
hawthorn trees, it was always a Friday in Lent. It was mass
before school. It was the Stations Of The Cross at 3 PM,
before going home from school. And there, in that grotto,
you could touch prayer beads of bark and thorns; and renew
your devotions in the cool darkness hidden in a summer day.
The smell of earth dying into earth, again and again. The Way
Of The Cross. The Way of Sorrows. It was the Sixth Station,
"Jesus is scourged and crowned with thorns." Outside, the
sun and the wind pushing warmth like low fi sound down the
sidewalk in front of my home and the field next to it, and the
rest of Lorain, Ohio.

The Marriage Of Murmur And Death

A dinner was hosted by Light and Darkness for the most beautiful and important words in the English language. Murmur and Death arrived a little late, and both were unaccompanied. Seeing this, Desire (the first-born daughter of Light and Darkness) was quick to seat them at the same table. It went well. They drank wine and nodded often. They laughed loudly, and whispered things to each other. Many noted that Ms. Murmur was seen smiling somewhat longingly at Death, as he excused himself and walked away to "speak briefly" with Hope and Fear who were eagerly waiting to know what he thought of his beautiful dinner partner. For years after the event, Desire told the story of her matchmaking in ever-lengthening detail. But then, it was hers to tell. After all, due to the quick seating plan of Desire, Murmur and Death were married just two months after the dinner. They had three children in relatively rapid succession, who they named Industry, Art, and Sleep. They were happy by most accounts, but then things changed. Death felt that their marriage was getting in the way of his job, and sued for divorce. Murmur did her best raising the children on her own, but there were difficulties, and rumors of drinking. Poets were neglecting her presence, and a cardiologist named a heart problem after her. Not long afterwards, Death was granted full custody of the children. Overwhelmed with sadness, she returned to her childhood home to live with her parents, Ineffable and Mellifluous. They were not surprised. They always considered Death to be selfish and crude and they were worried from the moment Murmur met him.

The Queen And The Book

The Queen, wearing a smart turquoise outfit, and haute couture turquoise hat, met with a man who wouldn't read. The meeting was official, and took place in the Queen's Palace. The man wore an unbuttoned blue suit coat and a red tie that descended below the belt and zipper of his massive blue suit pants. It was unclear why the Queen was required to attend to the presence of this man in her kingdom. He was notably vulgar. He lied and he played golf. The country he came from overthrew the rule of Kings and Queens. But there he was, in the Queen's Palace, speaking loudly and slapping the Queen on her back. The Court gasped. Then, recovering from his forbidden touching, she gifted the man a rare book, written by a Hero of the Kingdom. The Court gasped again. Louder. Why not an umbrella imprinted with the Queen's image? Why not a tea cup? Or a pencil touched by the Queen? But a book? A book of great value to a man who wouldn't read? Some said it was a mix-up in paperwork at the House of Lords, others feared it was a sign of the Queen's advanced age. But later, after the palace was scrubbed clean and new dinnerware was ordered, it dawned on everyone. It wasn't a gift at all. *It was a clever punishment!* Bells pealed. Lutes luted. And cheers of "God save the Queen!" erupted once again in homes and alehouses throughout the kingdom.

The Plus One, Minus Two Equation

Why are we afraid to say what we want? Because once said, and if rejected, life less the thing wanted is impossible. It's a plus one, minus two equation. The "declaration" of want will annihilate the status of the state of affairs up to that moment. What was accepted, the "less than" or "other than" in a relationship cannot be practiced after your voice releases the name of your desire. Saying what you want exposes the inferiority of what you've settled for, and eliminates it—*even if you're willing to continue that state of affairs.* We don't say what we want because we're afraid of losing everything we have. Including our own incompleteness.

Let's Say

A morning, let's say. A color, let's say amber, pulsing in a corner of somewhere. A voice revolves in ever-widening circles around your head. Let's say it's the voice of Thomas Edison testing his first phonograph. Then a note, handwritten on lilac colored paper slides under your shoe. You read it in the pulsing amber light. It says "Read only what you don't understand." Let's say you know you're somewhere you've never been before. Let's say you know you're never coming back.

INDEX OF LAST LINES

Border on wonder
These Small Frames

To someone else
The Three Of Her

Every echo forgets its beginning
AM Kindergarten 1959

We can see where things will end
The Distractions

Said I couldn't understand
In A Year Of Backward Glances

In their ears
The Early Birds

of the unknown
The Poles Bend Toward Each Other

until they hand you this
A Few Lines About Disappointment

Game over.
After Further Review

Without Saying
It Goes Without Saying

To enter our four lungs
Space Suites

There's nothing to return
The Lives Of The Silent

to sort out creation
Envelopes Of Words

And I don't want to.
The Patriot

Be grateful.
Prometheus v. Eve

"After so many shipwrecks, a haven."
Sir Real And The Earl Of Sandwich

though ultimately homeless place to be.
Where The Tears And The Antelope Play

Then, they were gone.
Then In The Neighborhood Of Love

Looking for a place to park.
Desire Never Gets A Snow day

I was never there…
Lunch With Michael Cohen In Prague

But the store stays open
Pushing Shopping Carts Around What's Left

—hoping no one notices
Discernment

"I'm not up for going
out tonight. You?"
Before You Said

Did you really go to work?
Questionnaire

That's why we whisper.
Seven Moon Poems

With the same person
Please Don't Hum

And when they do, it tastes like communion
Communion

I don't know what to do.
The Lost Key To The Grateful Room

That no one but you can see
Lips Closed

But nothing like this silence.
When You Didn't Respond

For your return.
The Bottom Of IT

See what you did there?
This Poem Differently

Come looking for you
Lost

leaking methane
All Day Cows

They had that same look
The Permissions Company

Of the unspoken inside us
Anniversary In Dallas

I was just trying to catch my breath
Snorkeling Through City Lights, San Francisco

doubt seemed to have disappeared.
Implanting The Appendix Of Understanding

And there you are.
And There You Are

It's up to you now
The Poetry Pogrom

But I was wrong; as I'm sure you can imagine.
Today's Date Minus 100 Years

we could see.
A View Resurrected

"I don't take your meaning," she said.
Different Meanings

to keep the colors in place.
The End Of The Movement

"Creativity," I said to myself.
Dark Matter

So it goes.
Warm Bricks And A Quick Disguise

in plain sight.
Uniforms

the lecture hasn't even begun.
The Lecture

was promptly hit and killed by a car that never stopped.
The Tale Of The Dogs

I never woke up.
I Never Woke Up

Our light blue, carbon-dated lives
Light Blue Advertising Agency

To be desired.
The Desired

Just to them
To Keep Us Silent

In that darkness
Ship In A Bottle

We all laugh, but no one says another word
What Once Was Home

But luckily, we have recordings
Mark Strand's Guitar

should delight and instruct
*Birthday Bash At Horace's
Place, December 8, 18 BC*

Two halves of the same possibility.
Frozen Fire Losses

Bethlehem
Orient-R

And we think back
What We Do Later

We'll have a laugh…
Not Another Poem About Death

Birth of desire
Green Jeep, Red Light

"Here is a song
for you"
After June 22, 1971

Take your time
First You Must Find A Wooden Piano

Hope to see you there
Out Of Order

By a thread
The Thread

Was that?
Mythology

What say you?
Then He Spoke

in branchless trees
Branchless Trees

The dog is long gone
The Man Six Stories Below Me

"thief!"
After The Doctor's Office

So small, parts of it never happened?
Waves Of Serenity

made with water from the River of Saudade
Dark Matter (II)

made a sound.
Dinner At One Hand Clapping

You said that? Yes.
The New Car Of Their Love

I hope I can pull it off.
Lines Written By A Bass Player

Talk to you soon.
Upbeat Emails From The Poem Family

the lights turn out to be a tanning bed.
The Third Professor Of The Day

And be closer to never again.
Close To Never Again

Yes, it is.
My Own Mistakes

Wanted more
Conjunctions

Every morning
The Easiest Thing In The World

Be Eve.
Poem On Writing Poems

We'll see. They'll see.
Experimental Phrases

Maybe it was a Wednesday
The Patient

And the line is backing up, and up and up
In Line At The UPS Store

Of lyric poetry
Sonnets

Forever...
Lexeme Dream

Did the nun know?
Wooden Desks

of their limbs
The Metronome And The Night Trees

You live. I only see the darkness.
Seven Window Poems

You've never seen
In The Dark

Or changing my address
November 2, Near Lake Erie

It's OK to arrive a little late, and laughing...
The Conestoga Wagon Of Perfection

before you give up your place.
Second Thoughts

Naked through Newark
The Obituaried Inventory Of Likes

In almost the same shoes
The Comparative Nature Of Names

—and became the 45th president.
Tempestuous

at me staring at you
Our New Names

in summer glare
A View From Above The Cleveland Yacht Club

"Burn these for warmth
Then show yourselves out."
The Lines Of Your Thinking

rest of Lorain, Ohio
The Way Of Sorrows

they were worried from the moment
Murmur met him.
The Marriage Of Murmur And Death

throughout the kingdom.
The Queen And The Book

Including our own incompleteness.
The Plus One, Minus Two Equation

you're never coming back.
Let's Say

ABOUT THE AUTHOR

Timothy Donohue's previous publications are *Road Frame Window: A Poetics Of Seeing* (2015), coauthored with Dennis Patrick Slattery and Donald Carlson, and *Invisible: Poems and Aphorisms* (2016). He is a native of Lorain, Ohio. In a professional career spanning four decades, he spent the first 20 years as a writer, producer and sometimes teacher of print and broadcast advertising. He spent the next 20 years as a managing administrator and Communications Director for non-profits dedicated to providing services to individuals with mental illness, developmental disabilities and chemical dependencies.